The Little Book with 50
BIG Ideas on
LEADERSHIP

Glenn Furuya

Copyright © 2011 Leadership Works, LLC / Glenn Furuya. Leadership Works is a registered trademark.

Copyright © 2012 by Simple Truths, LLC. Simple Truth is a registered trademark.

Published by Simple Truths, LLC, 1952 McDowell Road, Suite 300, Naperville, Illinois 60563
800-900-3427

All rights reserved. No portion of this book may be reproduced, stored in a retrieval system or transmitted in any form by any means—except for brief quotations in printed reviews—without the prior written permission of the publisher.

Editor: Howard E. Daniel

Photos: ShutterStock

Printed and bound in the United States of America

ISBN 978-1-60810-224-2

01 WOZ 13

Dedication

To the **Source** of all wisdom,
the many leaders who seek and
apply this wisdom, and the
positive difference they all make.

Table of Contents

Introduction

> "All truths are easy to understand once they are discovered;
> the point is to discover them."
> GALILEO GALILEI

Picture a huge pile of rocks and gravel, and think of it as all the world's accumulated knowledge on leadership. Now imagine scooping up the material with a shovel and sifting it all through a screen. Each scoop represents a book read, a workshop attended or wise counsel received from a practicing leader.

The largest rocks that are recovered—the most valuable nuggets—embody the 50 most powerful leadership ideas I've uncovered in 30 years of "digging" and "sifting."

I hope you will find the ideas in this book useful, memorable and stimulating. And, because leaders are busy people, I hope you will find this book a quick and easy read and one that you can often refer back to in your leadership journey.

With warm regards,

Glenn Furuya
President & CEO
Leadership Works

The True Essence of Leadership

Ka Makani

In Hawaiian, "Ka Makani" means "the wind."

Like a cool mountain breeze, real leaders uplift, invigorate and energize.

Others create effects more like devastating "hurricanes," depressing "doldrums," all-talk-no-action "hot air" and negative "break winds."

What kind of wind are you?

The Meaning of Leadership

The Big Why

The Big Why gives leadership meaning.
It's a compelling cause or a purposeful mission.

The Big Why focuses on serving the greater good and making a positive difference.

The Big Why engenders patience, tolerance, and persistence.

As Friedrich Nietzsche once said, "Given a big enough why, people can bear almost any how."

What's your "Big Why"?

Two Practical Outcomes of Leadership

ET

Remember the famous movie about the extraterrestrial, ET? Interestingly, these letters serve as a trigger for two practical and oppositional outcomes of leadership:

Efficacy and Transformation.

Efficacy concentrates on short-term results, such as achieving revenue goals, managing costs, boosting morale, ensuring compliance, and satisfying the customer.
It focuses on what happens today.

Paradoxically, transformation centers on building long-term success through organizational growth, product or service diversification and innovation and succession planning.
Transformation focuses on what happens tomorrow.

Real leaders can achieve both. Operationally, they can deliver high levels of quality, productivity and service, while simultaneously, they can strategically diversify operations, invest in new technologies, and develop new products and services to better meet their customers' needs.

Are you a high-efficacy, high-transformational leader?

A Defining Choice of Leadership

Wilt or Grow

> "There is no such thing as status quo.
> You either wilt or grow."
>
> UNKNOWN

Poor leadership results in failure and decline.
Real leadership produces success and growth.

*Choose to **GROW!***

The Lasting Mark
of Leadership

Colors and Textures

"The true worth of a man is not to be found in man himself, but in **the colors and textures that come alive in others.**"

ALBERT SCHWEITZER

What "colors and textures" does your leadership bring out in others?

Inspired employees?
Harmonious team players?
Efficient systems?
Happy customers?
A growing organization?

What are the "colors and textures"
of your leadership?

The Distinctive Sound of Leadership

Resonance

Strike a chime and hear it resonate.

Beautiful sounds radiate from it, filling the air.

Real leaders radiate too.

They radiate a positive spirit,

which makes people feel good.

Sadly, like the thump of a fist hitting a wall,

others radiate dissonance—anger, apathy, abuse.

To resonate harmoniously, simply approach everyone as if they were volunteers. Imagine they have come to help you free of charge, out of the goodness of their hearts.

How do you treat a volunteer?

With respect, clarity, consideration and appreciation! When you treat people like volunteers, they work harder, make that extra effort, deliver outstanding service, and show you long-term loyalty.

How do you resonate as a leader?

The Starting Point of Leadership

Mindfulness

"Consciousness is the
source of your ability.
Learn to be
increasingly conscious."

LAO TZU

Open your eyes.
Open your ears.
It will open your mind.

*Are you alert, attentive
and present?*

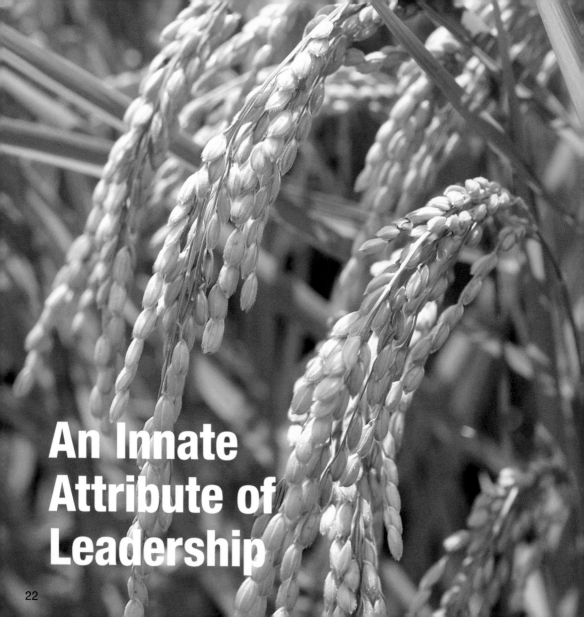

An Innate Attribute of Leadership

Humility

It has been said that the quality of a field of rice can be determined by how low the stalks bend to the ground. The lower they bend, the better the quality (plumper grains weigh the stalks down more).

Similarly, real leaders "bend low." Appreciating people, they proceed with sincerity and humility.

Recognizing their own shortcomings, they listen attentively and continuously seek to improve.

Are you a humble leader?

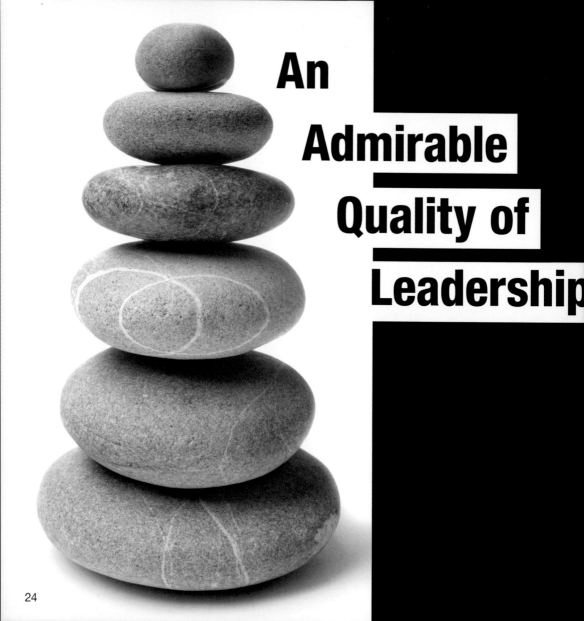

An Admirable Quality of Leadership

Centeredness

Buddha once said, "The great rock is not disturbed by the wind. Neither is the mind of a wise man (or woman) disturbed by either honor or abuse."

When confronted by difficult people or thorny situations, real leaders stay centered.
Rather than "fight or flee," they...

Stop

Think

Decide

Do

To start the **STDD** process, stay centered and call "time out."

Are you like the "great rock"?

here Leaders Go to Thin

The Zone

Between stimulus and response lies a place called the "zone." Instead of giving in to typical "fight or flight" impulses, real leaders enter this space to deliberately choose their responses. Their actions then come across as composed, reasonable and honorable.

Decisions are based on criteria. The walls of the "zone" serve as the guidelines for your choices:

- Which choice best comports with my life's purpose?
- Which choice best aligns with my life's principles?
- Which choice makes the most sense in light of my education and experience?

Do you sometimes let your instincts rule, or do you take full advantage of the "zone"?

The Sparkplug
for Motivation

A Singing Heart!

> "Choose a job you love and you'll never work another day in your life."
>
> CONFUCIUS

Real leaders have two key challenges:

First, find what makes your heart sing by discovering your gifts and talents.

Second, help others find what makes their hearts sing.

Place people in jobs that bring them joy and set them up to succeed.

Does your heart sing?

An Intriguing Paradox of Leadership

Two Think®

"Two Think" is a revolutionary mindset and approach to leadership. It challenges leaders to embrace contradictory and paradoxical thoughts and behaviors and blend them in order to achieve higher levels of communication, teamwork and success.

Real leadership often requires simultaneous focus on opposing factors, such as:

Short-term + Long-term

People + Results

High service + Low cost

Individual effort + Team interdependence

Risk + Reward

Think "both/and," not "either/or."

Are you a "Two Think" leader?

The Four
Voices of
Leadership

Empathy, Drive, Passion and Reason

Real leaders speak in two pairs of sometimes contradictory voices:
Empathy & Drive and Passion & Reason. They employ these four
voices appropriately, depending on the situation they
face or the person they are working with.

EMPATHY
The voice of empathy reflects a leader's concern for people.
It embodies humility, compassion and cooperation.

DRIVE
The voice of drive reflects a leader's desire for results.
It shows up as direction, organization and control.
Using these often contradictory voices, real leaders get the job done
thanks to their ability to inspire people.

PASSION
The voice of passion personifies a leader's eagerness to inspire others and
fervor in a cause. Passion sparks enthusiasm, creativity and commitment.

REASON
The voice of reason addresses a leader's need for order and precision.
Reason elicits clarity, organization and accuracy.

Using these four voices, real leaders inspire people to serve, through
systems that foster precision and consistency.

Are you a "four voice" leader?

The Toughest Challenge of Leadership

Knowing and Managing Oneself

Leaders are like cars.

First, put your car in "drive."
Know where you're going.
Identify your life's goals.

Release the parking brake.
Neutralize your weaknesses.

Step on the gas.
Accentuate your strengths.
Develop your talents.

Steer attentively.
Life is a winding road.

The toughest challenge of leadership
is to lead oneself.

Moving forward?

A "Fountain of Youth" for Leaders

Neoteny

Legend has it that Spanish explorer Ponce de Leon sought the Fountain of Youth, whose waters were said to cure aging.

Real leaders have discovered that **neoteny** can be a genuine "Fountain of Youth."

"Neoteny" refers to childlike qualities retained in adulthood. Love, creativity and curiosity are such positive qualities.

These qualities are essential to leaders.
Love generates support, loyalty endorsement.
Creativity brings about new ideas and better ways.
Curiosity results in continual learning and limitless personal growth.

Got neoteny?

The Bonding Glue
of Leadership

TRUST

Like glue,
trust bonds people
together.

Commitment and
loyalty emerge
from trust.

*Do your people
trust you?*

Three Ways to Build Trust

The Three "RITY"

Three words that end in the letters **"rity"**
form the basis for trust.

ChaRITY

People will trust you when they "feel"
your selfless, giving ways.
With charity, they trust your "heart."

ClaRITY

People trust leaders who provide a clear vision,
relevant instruction and good information.
With clarity, they trust your "head."

IntegRITY

People trust leaders who walk their talk,
live their beliefs and keep their promises.
With integrity, they trust your "character" and your "word."

Which "RITY" do you need to work on?

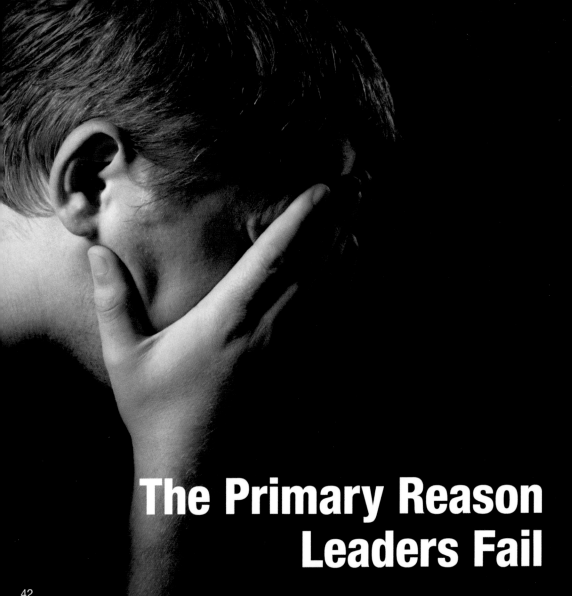

The Primary Reason
Leaders Fail

Working IN vs. Working ON

Two little words, IN and ON, could spell the difference between success and failure in leadership.

Those who work IN are caught in the frenzy of task inundation, bombarded with technical work, administrative chores and a never-ending stream of complaints. They "run around like headless chickens," spending little or no time improving systems or empowering people.

Leaders who work ON rise above the flurry of these activities and dedicate time to focus, plan, organize, coordinate, communicate and mentor. Instead of reacting to problems, they work proactively to prevent them. By working ON, real leaders improve and grow their organizations.

Are you working ON?

Two Vital
Leadership
Systems

Two systems run in every organization.
A duck and its feet best illustrate them.

The Duck

Think of your organization like a duck in a pond. The duck represents system 1, your operations. The duck's feet, or system 2, symbolize work ON activities previously mentioned. When the duck's feet paddle consistently and uniformly, the bird glides smoothly forward. If the feet move irregularly or remain still, the result of working IN, the duck moves erratically or makes no forward progress.

The Duck's Two Feet

Each of the duck's feet stands for a critical "work ON" element of leadership. The left foot represents rituals— regular activities conducted by leaders, such as huddles, one-on-one sessions, annual planning sessions and debriefings. The right foot corresponds to a leader's behavior, which sets the tone for "working ON" and serves as an example for everyone.

Does your duck swim straight?

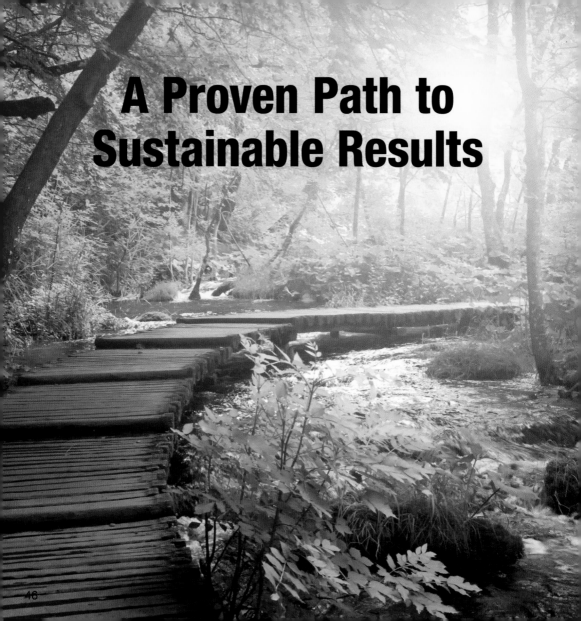

A Proven Path to Sustainable Results

Believe in and practice

The Leadership Mantra

Systems make it possible.
People make it happen.
Leadership is the key.

To achieve sustainable results...

Optimize your **systems.**
Empower your **people.**
Strengthen your **leadership.**

What results are you achieving?

An Unlikely
Leadership Mascot

The Starfish

The starfish represents a critical metaphor for leadership. The starfish symbolizes your team and each arm, the various interacting departments. At the center of the starfish is a "nerve ring," which connects each arm of the starfish and controls its movement by sending and receiving signals through the nerves that run along its arms.

For example, when the tiny "light sensors" of the starfish's arms detect an approaching predator or a nearby food source, a message is sent to the "nerve ring," which then coordinates the arms, making some push and others pull in the desired direction.

Like a starfish, leaders serve as the "nerve ring" of their organizations, communicating key information, directing activities and establishing unity. Without an effective "nerve ring," team members often operate in "silos," failing to properly communicate, coordinate and align themselves to common goals.

How effective is your "nerve ring"?

The Three Most Important Words of Leadership

Talk to Me

Honor your people by inviting them
to share ideas, vent concerns and
establish a relationship.

Begin by saying, "Talk to me."

Listening makes people feel important,
intelligent and valued.

They'll repay you by putting forth
their best effort.

Are you a good listener?

The Official Drink
of Leadership

Tea

"Hot water" connotes difficulty, pain and suffering. When you're in hot water, you have choices....

You can be a carrot.
Place a carrot in hot water. Let it boil for 10 minutes and the carrot softens and goes limp. Like a carrot, weak leaders complain, whine and give up.

You can be a hard-boiled egg.
Place an egg in hot water.
Let it boil for 10 minutes and the egg gets hard.
Like an egg, weak leaders become upset,
heated and abusive.

Avoid these choices.

Make Tea!
Place a tea bag in "hot water" and it becomes a refreshing drink. Real leaders turn negatives into positives by making "tea."

"(People) are like tea bags, you never know how strong they are until they get into hot water."

ELEANOR ROOSEVELT

Is it "tea" time?

A Pivot Point for Improvement

Think Like An Auditor

When problems and drama occur, real leaders immediately assemble the team to assess the situation and plan corrective measures.

When conducting such an assessment, think like an auditor and ask yourself the following questions:

Is there a protocol?
Is the protocol effective?
Are people following the protocol?

If you answer "no" to any of these questions, determine how to keep the problem from arising again.

Is there an "audit" you need to conduct?

A Smart Leadership Investment

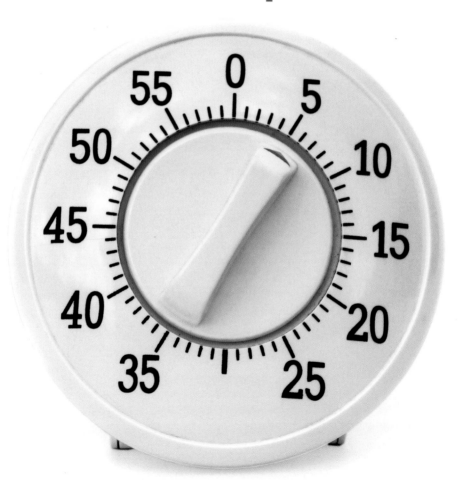

The First Five Minutes
(of your day)

Start smart.
Meet and greet.
Set a positive mood.
Call the "plays."
Communicate and coordinate.
Listen to concerns.
Celebrate victories.

A small investment that yields big returns.

Do you start smart?

A Healthy Leadership Ritual

An APPLE Briefing

Acknowledge
- Thank.
- Recognize positive behaviors and performance.

Plan and **P**revent
- Set goals, organize, orchestrate and communicate.
- Anticipate and plan for potential problems.

Listen and teach a **L**esson
- Listen to concerns and ideas.
- Provide feedback and mentoring, teaching mini-lessons.

Emphasize and **E**nergize
- Reinforce team vision and values.
- End on a positive, inspirational note.

An APPLE a day keeps the DRAMA away!

A Basic Leadership Skill

Read, Shed and Respond

Like a football linebacker, defending the opposing offense from scoring touchdowns, real leaders must be able to appropriately **read, shed** and **respond.**

To **"read"** is to be present, aware and attentive to the needs of your organization.

To **"shed"** is to avoid being distracted from achieving your goals by low priority administrative tasks and unnecessary interruptions.

To **"respond"** is to take appropriate action to solve problems, eliminate threats and leverage opportunities.

What kind of "linebacker" are you?

Two Essential Shapes of Leadership

Circular and Linear

Circular leadership focuses on people, emphasizing inclusion, collaboration and interdependence.

Linear leadership concentrates on tasks and getting the job done. The linear approach requires focus, order and independent action.

Circular-only leaders often fail to deliver results. Linear-only leaders can trigger dissension and resistance.

Real leaders employ both approaches. They combine circular preparation with linear execution.

Are you a circular-linear leader, combining the best of both approaches?

How Leaders Get Going

They GO slow to GO fast!

"Go slow" means taking time to think, focus, plan, organize, communicate, listen and teach.

"Go fast" shows up as flawless execution, delivered by a well-aligned team, "ready, willing and able" to get the job done.

Unfortunately, some hurriedly choose to "go fast without starting slow," resulting in mistakes, rework, confusion and low morale.

As the Navy Seals say, "Slow is smooth. Smooth is fast."

How do you go?

A Leadership Lesson from Aesop

The Goose and the Golden Egg

In the famous Aesop Fable, a greedy couple who owned a goose that laid golden eggs killed the goose to harvest their bounty all at once. They butchered the source of their wealth but found no eggs.

The moral of the story for real leaders?

The golden eggs represent results. The goose represents the people and systems that produce the golden eggs.

Nurture the goose by building better systems and growing your people. The golden eggs will come.

*How well are you caring for **your** goose?*

Two Core Elements of Teamwork

Individual Effort and Interdependence

Coaches often try to galvanize their teams with the famous saying *"there is no "i" in team."* They do this to emphasize the importance of cooperation and a team-first approach, trying to encourage team members to put their egos aside and focus on "we," not "me."

Leaders, however, believe that the letter "i," although not in the word "team," is critical for teamwork and represents two key elements of a peak performer.

The first "i" denotes the need for "individual effort." The best team members work hard, pull their weight and make a positive difference.

The second "i" signifies the need for "interdependence." Effective team members cooperate, help out and get along with others.

Teamwork evolves when everyone minds their "i"s.

Do you have "teiiamwork"?

A Unifying Cheer

AFOOFA!

Like the "Three Musketeers,"
team players practice **AFOOFA!**

All **F**or **O**ne **O**ne **F**or **A**ll

*Does your team exhibit
"AFOOFA" behaviors?*

Two Key Qualities of a Peak Performer

Skill and Will

A peak performer has two key qualities:

Skill, or competence, is the ability to perform a task correctly and in a timely manner.

Will, or commitment, is the eagerness, energy and spirit shown in the way tasks are done.

Skill and will are task-specific. Different tasks may produce varying degrees of skill and will.

Note that in skill and will, you find the word "ill."

When a team member fails to perform up to expectations, ask: Is the *ill* in the sk*ill* or is the *ill* in the w*ill*?

If the **ill** is in the sk**ill**, provide direction: Explain, teach, demonstrate and supervise.

If the **ill** is in the w**ill**, provide support: Listen, reassure, encourage, prioritize and mediate.

Are you developing peak performers?

You Can't Lead
Without It!

A Bowl of Fruit

Imagine a bowl of fruit. The bowl symbolizes expectations, values, standards, policies and protocols.

The fruit represents team members, meeting expectations and behaving appropriately.

Now, picture a banana falling out of the fruit bowl. A "banana" represents anyone who behaves inappropriately or fails to meet performance expectations.

Teams function best when everyone knows and follows the rules.

Leaders must clearly and routinely define the bowl to minimize negative outcomes and potential "banana" behaviors.

How well-defined is your "bowl"?

Why Leaders Need Courage

To Handle Bananas

Real leaders muster the courage to confront "bananas." They respectfully place truth over harmony to promptly address poor performance and unacceptable behaviors.

Weak leaders, on the other hand, hesitate to be forthright and truthful because they are afraid "to rock the boat." Fearful of retribution, they avoid confrontation, creating confusion and an "implied consent" that those behaviors are acceptable. It diminishes a leader's credibility and effectiveness.

Are you handling your "bananas"?

How Leaders Keep

People

in the Bowl

RRRR

Rules, Reminders, Rewards, Redirection

RULES
Rules define what people can and cannot do.
Set clear rules.

REMINDERS
Regularly review and reinforce the rules.

REWARDS
Acknowledge and praise compliance with the rules.

REDIRECTION
Immediately correct poor performance
and address improper behaviors.

Which "R" do you need to work on?

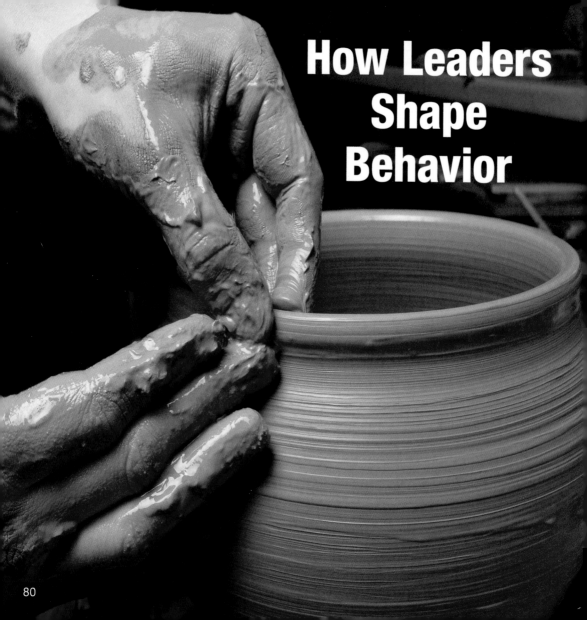

How Leaders Shape Behavior

ABC

Getting people to behave as you
want is as simple as **ABC**.

Activate behaviors
Set clear expectations, inspire, teach.

Behave as you'd like others to do
Serve as a model for desired behaviors.

Commend
Praise examples of desired behaviors.

If a desired behavior fails to manifest itself,
re-**A**ctivate.

*Do you know your **ABCs**?*

Three Things Leaders Get from Their People

The Behaviors You Exhibit
The Behaviors You Reward
The Behaviors You Tolerate

You get back from your people the behaviors
you exhibit, reward and tolerate.

Behaviors you demonstrate recur.
Behaviors you praise repeat.
Behaviors you allow persist.

What are you getting?

How Leaders
Stay Connected

LBWA
Lead By Walking Around

Real leaders operate at the "grass-roots" level, maintaining high visibility and accessibility.

This gives them a better perspective of what is happening, the effectiveness of their systems and the well-being of their people.

It keeps them in touch and helps them listen better and see things first-hand.

Team members view leaders who **LBWA** as humble, concerned and connected.

When's the last time you left your office?

How Leaders View the World

Whole-listically

If you look at your hand through the small hole of a funnel, you see your entire hand. Dr. W. Edwards Deming referred to this as the **"whole-listic" view.**

Conversely, if you look at your hand through the large hole of the funnel, you only see the tip of one finger. Dr. Deming called this an **"analytic"** view.

These are the two perspectives leaders get as they look at their organizations. Both are necessary, but real leaders start with the "whole-listic" perspective. They see their organizations, like a hand, as interdependent parts working together to get the job done. Unfortunately, many leaders approach their organizations "analytically," resulting in independent and divided silos.

What's your view?

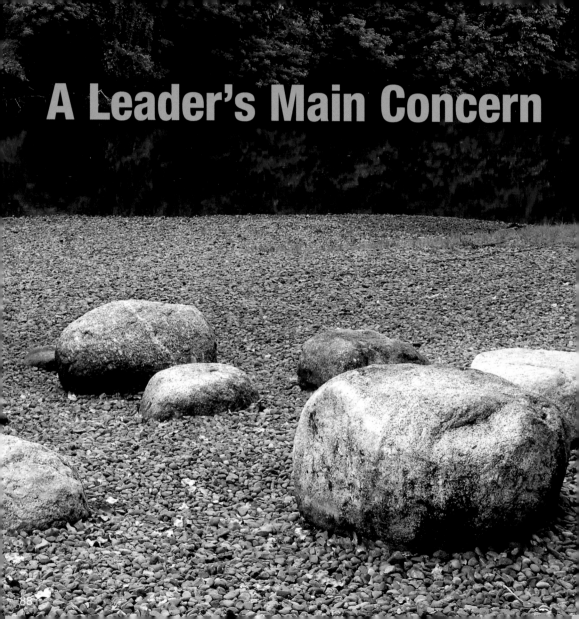

A Leader's Main Concern

Big Rocks First

As Stephen Covey points out, "big rocks" are the most important things in life, like God, family and living healthily. Leadership "big rocks" include planning, communication, coordination, education and listening.

"Pebbles" symbolize life's many mundane activities, such as commuting, cleaning, laundry and television. In leadership, "pebbles" include e-mail, filing, time sheets and unfocused meetings.

Leaders always put "big rocks" first, never sacrificing the "vital few" for the "trivial many." As Goethe wrote, "The things that matter most must never be at the mercy of the things that matter least."

Are you putting "big rocks" first?

How Leaders Get Things Done

Flag on Path

Imagine a path of stepping stones. The path represents your life, and each stepping stone represents a day.

Now picture a stepping stone farther down the path with a flag planted on it. As you walk the path, you get to the flag and it seizes your attention.

Leaders apply this "flag on path" method to get things done. Appointment books, cell phones and electronic calendars lay out the path. "Flags" are the "to-do" entries, including daily chores, steps of a plan and rituals. "Flags on path" trigger actions.

When "flags" appear, real leaders arrive at "match point," where walk meets talk. By taking action at "match point," things get done and credibility is strengthened.

Are you winning at "match point"?

How Leaders Get to Excellence

Take On-ramp "superVISION"

"Everything is created twice, first in the mind." UNKNOWN

"SuperVISION" is a picture of operational perfection. It's a portrait of people, processes, products, equipment and place in the ideal state. It's a clear definition of excellence.

To create this vision, just fill in the blank:
"I see a place where _____."

Real leaders ensure that all team members have superVISION.

To create superVISION, first develop it yourself. Then get team members involved. Make it compelling, engaging and visual.

Once superVISION is established, mind sensors (antenna) will automatically start picking up anything that doesn't fit the vision of perfection. Walt Disney referred to these imperfections as "wispy tendrils." Wispy tendrils are little roots. If you were to pluck them, they readily break off. Walt Disney believed that problems are similar to these roots and if you handle them when they are small, they can be resolved with little effort. By constantly seeking out and correcting wispy tendrils real leaders progress, step by step, toward operational perfection.

Got superVISION?

A Critical Leadership Obligation

Bifurcation

W. Edwards Deming once asked, "Are you building carburetors?" It's a critical question that leaders must continually ask, in light of how fast the world is changing. A carburetor is a device that blends air and fuel in an automobile engine. Decades ago, carburetors began to be replaced by "fuel injection" systems, a much-improved way of blending air and fuel.

If a company today built only carburetors, it would be forced to refocus, diversify or die, since the vast majority of automobiles now use fuel injection.

For this reason, bifurcation is a critical leadership obligation. Bifurcation means splitting something into two parts. For real leaders, "splitting" means transforming their organizations to avoid irrelevance and obsolescence. It means beginning to move to fuel injection long before demand for carburetors evaporates.

Hockey legend Wayne Gretzky once said, " I skate to where the puck is going to be, not where it has been." Likewise, real leaders intuitively anticipate paradigm shifts and changing customer/client/consumer needs. Strategic anticipation precedes bifurcation.

Are you building carburetors?
Are you skating to where the puck is going to be?
Are you anticipating and bifurcating in time
to avoid obsolescence?

How Leaders Boost Productivity

Think Like a Wood Chopper

To boost productivity, think of your team members as **wood choppers** and consider the following questions:

Are the right team members assigned to chop the wood?
Do they have the skill and will?

Do team members know what standards they must achieve?
What does good chopped wood look like?
How much wood needs to be chopped in a given time frame?

Do team members have the right tools? Are the tools well maintained?
Is the ax sharp? Should you invest in a chain saw?

Do team members have the proper safety equipment?
Goggles, gloves?

Have team members been properly trained on how to use the tools?
What's the best way to chop?

Are conditions like space, temperature, organization and cleanliness conducive to high productivity?
Is there enough room to swing an ax?

Have unnecessary bottlenecks, movement and travel been minimized so work flows smoothly?
Is the wood staged next to the chopping block and is the storage area nearby?

Are team members treated respectfully?
Everyone treated like a volunteer?

Do team members get feedback on their performance and behaviors?
"Bananas" promptly and respectfully addressed?

How to Create Enduring Harmony

Pass Nicely!

Because he believed in linear flow, Dr. W. Edwards Deming considered the "next process" as everyone's customer.

Department to department or person to person, everyone passes work one to another until it reaches the consumer.

Everyone must then do anything and everything possible to facilitate the work of the person or group to whom they are passing their own work. This simple and considerate gesture goes a long way to building goodwill among team members and better serving the customer.

Failure to do this causes lots of drama.

Is everyone passing nicely?

How Leaders Gain Customer Trust and Loyalty

Deliver Quality

According to Dr. W. Edwards Deming, quality involves several key factors. First and foremost, all effort must focus on creating customer joy. Positive reactions from customers come from delivering a cake, with frosting and a cherry on top.

The cake represents a solution. Every organization exists primarily to solve a problem. Supermarkets relieve hunger. Teachers create literacy. An insurance company provides a sense of security. Police fight crime. Cake is key. Many successful organizations, such as big-box retailers, are built on a "cake-only" formula.

Frosting corresponds to good feelings. Friendly greetings, heartfelt helpfulness, and sincere appreciation elicit happy responses.

The cherry on top refers to "lagniappe," or the provision of an "unexpected something extra." Customers respond by saying, "Wow!"

The best organizations deliver all three – cake, frosting and cherry.

The second critical factor for quality, according to Dr. Deming, is consistency. This is achieved by reducing/eliminating "variation."

If an organization's service process is to "greet, help and thank," everyone on the team must do so. Variation occurs when someone fails to say "hello," responds coldly to a request for assistance, or forgets to say "thank you." Manufacturing operations have sophisticated methods to minimize variation in their production to yield a highly reliable product.

When "cake, frosting and cherry" are presented consistently, predictability results. With this sense of certainty, customer trust and loyalty develop.

Are you delivering quality?

A Painful Trap
to Avoid

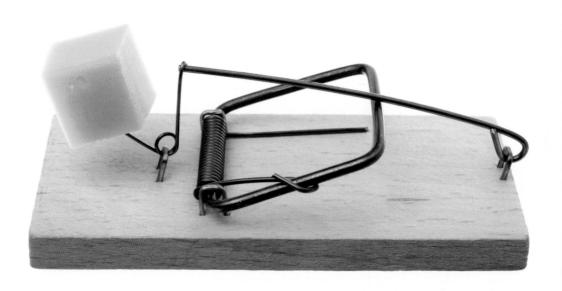

Lack of Discipline

Discipline is…
Doing what needs to be done,
even if you really don't want to do it.
(Example: Addressing misbehavior)

Not doing what you shouldn't,
even if you really want to.
(Example: Not reacting angrily
to someone who misbehaves)

These are two sides of the same coin –
letting your emotions get in the
way of your better judgment.

How disciplined are you?

The Curse of
Poor Leadership

Drama!

Ineffective systems, disempowered people and poor leadership produce **drama**!

Drama manifests itself as customer complaints and employee grievances. **Drama** shows up as conflicts, flareups and passive-aggressive behavior.

With smooth-running systems, operated by competent, committed people, well-led organizations have very little **drama.**

*Got **drama**?*

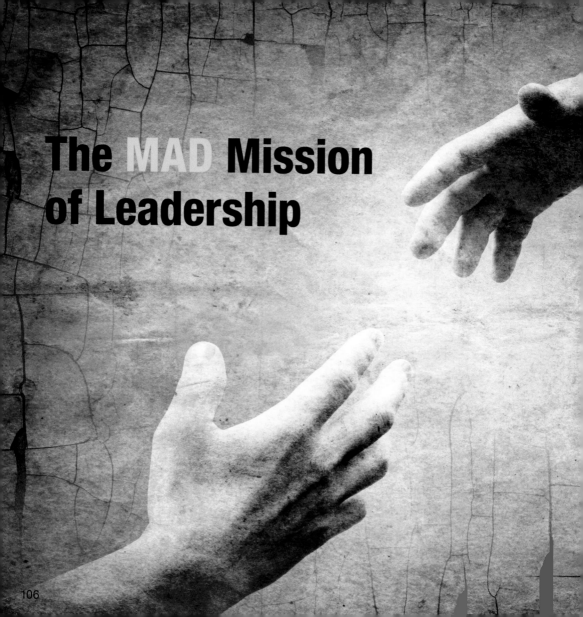

The MAD Mission of Leadership

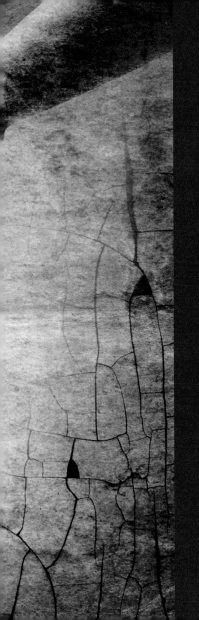

Make
A
Difference!

Conclusion

An experienced painter prepares a surface for painting by first applying a coat of primer. With this foundational base, the finish coat sticks better, lasts longer and looks nicer. This produces superior results and saves both time and money in the long run.

The 50 leadership lessons shared in this book represent a primer for leadership. Over the past three decades, I've been honored to share these ideas with thousands of individuals and hundreds of organizations. Along the way, I've received numerous thank you cards and e-mails from people, who have shared with me how these lessons positively impacted their lives. I kept each and every one.

Some are from individuals who applied what they learned and created a successful business entity, some shared how the lessons helped them build better relationships with their families, and some simply stated how they were able to chart a new path to fulfillment.

Like the personal testimonies I've received, I hope you'll find that the 50 little leadership ideas shared in this book will yield big results, whatever your endeavor.

Practice these simple leadership truths and you'll optimize systems, empower your people and grow your leadership.

About the Author

Glenn Furuya is the founder, president and CEO of Leadership Works, Hawaii's leading business development and consulting company in the areas of leadership and professional development, personal empowerment, and organizational transformation. It is an organization that has been devoted to growing people, teams and businesses for more than three decades!

Born and raised in Hilo, Hawaii, Glenn's Eastern heritage, island upbringing and Western education form a unique three-way blend—a confluence of ideologies that is critical for success in today's global economy.

With Bachelor and Master Degrees in Education from the University of Hawaii, Glenn started his career as a special education teacher, an eight-year journey that he says really taught him to lead. Faced with a classroom of adolescent children, many with severe mental and emotional disabilities, Glenn created strategies and fostered an environment that inspired these children to learn. As such, he was recognized as one of Hawaii's "Outstanding Young Educators."

During this time, Glenn also served as the head of advertising and assistant to the company president at KTA Super Stores, a family-owned grocery chain on the Big Island of Hawaii. There he gained valuable business experiences and insights as a key member of a team tasked with transforming the organization from a small, family-owned market to a modern retail entity.

In 1982, armed with profound knowledge in both education and business, Glenn left his teaching position and job at KTA to pursue his passion in leadership and formed Leadership Works.

Glenn is a certified Social Style and Hay Assessment trainer, has trained with some of the top seminar and business leaders of our time, including Dr. W. Edwards Deming—the father of the quality movement in Japan, and has worked side-by-side with numerous leaders and organizations of all sizes and industries. His extensive knowledge in leadership and process improvement, energetic and engaging method of teaching and his ability to reach across cultures has made him one of the top leadership experts and educators in his field.

Leadership Works offers a distinctive approach to developing leaders through consulting, speeches and a multitude of leadership workshops, including its signature course, "The Leadership Works Experience."

For more information visit www.leadershipworks.com

If you have enjoyed this book we invite you to check out our entire collection of gift books, with free inspirational movies, at www.simpletruths.com. You'll discover it's a great way to inspire friends and family, or to thank your best customers and employees.

For more information, please visit us at:

www.simpletruths.com

Or call us toll free... **800-900-3427**